Totally AMAZING FACTS ABOUT DOGS

NIKKI POTTS

CAPSTONE PRESS
a capstone imprint

DOGS HAVE BEEN DOMESTICATED FOR AT LEAST 15,000 YEARS.

They are **DESCENDANTS of** GRAY WOLVES.

There are MORE than 400 DOG BREEDS.

THE UNITED STATES HAS MORE DOGS THAN ANY OTHER COUNTRY.

DOGS WERE ONCE BANNED AS PETS IN ICELAND.

I OBJECT!

THERE ARE NEARLY 90 MILLION PET DOGS IN THE USA.

 THEY ARE KEPT AS PETS IN MANY PARTS OF THE WORLD.

But in **SOME** countries, dogs are used for **FOOD!**

Say **WHAT?!**

9

SOME WAYS PEOPLE FIRST USED DOGS WERE FOR **HUNTING** AND **PROTECTION.**

When livestock became DOMESTICATED, dogs HERDED and PROTECTED them as well.

DOGS CAN LEARN UP TO 250 WORDS.

The Daily Dog News

The average dog thinks like a 2-YEAR-OLD.

13

SOME DOGS ARE ABLE TO SMELL AND IDENTIFY CANCER IN HUMANS.

MAX IS THE MOST POPULAR MALE DOG NAME.

BELLA IS THE MOST POPULAR FEMALE DOG NAME.

DOGS HAVE A BASIC UNDERSTANDING OF MATH.

THE GERMAN SHEPHERD IS THE TOP POLICE AND MILITARY DOG BREED.

OFFICER WOOF, reporting for duty.

The movie *Megan Leavey* is based on a TRUE STORY about a U.S. MARINE and her COMBAT DOG, SERGEANT REX.

A DOG HAS

200-300

MILLION

SCENT RECEPTORS
IN ITS NOSE.

A DOG CAN SMELL AT LEAST 1,000 TIMES BETTER THAN A HUMAN.

Like HUMANS, DOGS can have seasonal ALLERGIES.

ACHOO!

A dog's brain releases the "happy chemical," **OXYTOCIN,** when spending time with some humans and other dogs.

Life is pretty **AWESOME** right now!

DOGS CAN ALSO FEEL JEALOUS!

DOGS HAVE AROUND 1,700 TASTE BUDS.

HUMANS HAVE ABOUT 9,000!

THE **WETNESS** OF A DOG'S NOSE IS ACTUALLY A **THIN LAYER** OF MUCUS.

THE WETNESS HELPS THE DOG **SMELL.**

A DOG'S NORMAL BODY TEMPERATURE IS **101–102.5** DEGREES FAHRENHEIT (38.3–39.2 DEGREES CELSIUS).

A small dog's heart BEATS between 100–140 TIMES PER MINUTE.

OVER 40% OF DOGS SLEEP IN BED WITH THEIR OWNERS.

ALMOST 70% of dog owners think their **DOG KNOWS** when a **STORM** is coming.

A SPECIAL MEMBRANE IN A DOG'S EYES HELPS IT SEE AT NIGHT.

THE MEMBRANE IS CALLED THE

TAPETUM LUCIDUM.

DO YOUR DOG'S PAWS SMELL LIKE CORN CHIPS OR POPCORN?

PUPPIES CAN SLEEP AS MUCH AS 20 HOURS A DAY!

They are also born DEAF and BLIND.

DOGS HAVE ABOUT 320 BONES!

PUPPIES have 28 TEETH.

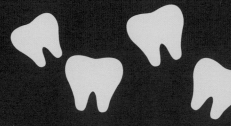

ADULT dogs have 42 TEETH.

IT IS A NATURAL INSTINCT FOR DOGS TO SPIN BEFORE LYING DOWN. DOGS NATURALLY CURL UP WHEN THEY SLEEP.

Z Z ZZZZ

This position **PROTECTS** vital organs and keeps dogs **WARM.**

A dog can SENSE a person's ANXIETY.

PETTING A DOG CAN LOWER YOUR BLOOD PRESSURE.

MOCHI THE ST. BERNARD HOLDS THE WORLD RECORD FOR LONGEST DOG TONGUE AT 7.31 INCHES (18.58 CENTIMETERS) LONG.

An **AUSTRALIAN CATTLE DOG** named **BLUEY** lived to **29 YEARS** and **5 MONTHS** old.

CONGRATULATIONS

He holds the world record for **OLDEST DOG.**

51

BASENJIS HAVE BEEN HANGING OUT WITH HUMANS FOR A LONG TIME!

IN FACT, SOME PEOPLE SAY BASENJIS WERE GIVEN TO EGYPTIAN PHARAOHS AS GIFTS.

WOOO! AWWOOO!

BASENJIS DON'T BARK—THEY YODEL!

The WORLD'S SHORTEST dog is a CHIHUAHUA named MILLY.

At just
3.8 INCHES
(9.7 CENTIMETERS)
TALL,

she's shorter than a CAN OF SODA!

NORWEGIAN LUNDEHUNDS HAVE **SIX TOES** ON EACH FOOT.

They can **CLOSE THEIR EARS** and **TIP THEIR HEADS**

ALL THE WAY BACK.

A GREAT PYRENEES NAMED DUKE WON THE MAYORAL ELECTION THREE TIMES RUNNING IN CORMORANT, MINNESOTA.

NEWFOUNDLANDS

HAVE WEBBED FEET!

They are also known as "Newfies."

Dalmatian puppies are born all WHITE!

64

They develop their **SPOTS** later on in life.

A BORDER COLLIE NAMED CHASER IS THOUGHT TO BE THE WORLD'S SMARTEST DOG.

SHE RECOGNIZES THE NAMES OF MORE THAN 1,000 OBJECTS!

ORIENT, A GERMAN SHEPHERD GUIDE DOG, successfully led his BLIND OWNER through the APPALACHIAN TRAIL.

The trek took 8 MONTHS.

DOGS CAN BE TRAINED TO HELP PEOPLE WHO ARE HAVING SEIZURES.

They lie next to their owners to PREVENT INJURY.

Dogs have at least
18 MUSCLES
in each ear.

THEY CAN SHUT OFF THEIR INNER EAR TO DROWN OUT DISTRACTING SOUNDS.

73

BASSET HOUNDS

have some of the **LONGEST EARS** of any breed.

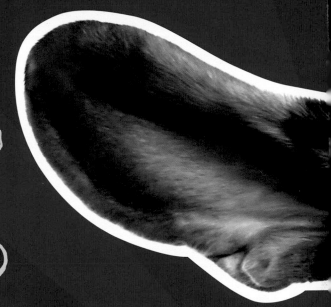

If I flap them hard enough, do you think **I COULD FLY?!**

SOME MEASURE
10 INCHES
(25.4 CENTIMETERS)
LONG!

A SERVICE DOG NAMED KIRSCH RECEIVED AN HONORARY DEGREE FROM JOHNS HOPKINS UNIVERSITY.

(HE ATTENDED EVERY CLASS WITH HIS OWNER, CARLOS.)

DOGS CAN HEAR SOUNDS OF 35,000 VIBRATIONS PER SECOND.

HUMANS CAN ONLY HEAR

20,000

VIBRATIONS PER SECOND.

It's said that the BRUSSELS GRIFFON breed was the inspiration for EWOK characters in the STAR WARS movies.

POMERANIANS

WEIGH JUST 7-10 POUNDS
(3.2-4.5 KILOGRAMS).

That's about the same weight as the average watermelon.

A **CHIWEENIE**
is a cross between a
CHIHUAHUA and a **DACHSHUND.**

ALTHOUGH SMALL, CHIWEENIES **BARK** TO PROTECT LOVED ONES. THEY CAN BE GREAT WATCHDOGS!

MANNY THE FRENCHIE IS A FAMOUS FRENCH BULLDOG.

He gained popularity on INSTAGRAM, where his owner POSTED pictures of him SNOOZING IN A SINK.

HE WAS NAMED ONE OF THE MOST INFLUENTIAL PETS IN 2017.

DOGS HAVE SOME SWEAT GLANDS IN THEIR PAWS.

But **PANTING** is their main way of **COOLING OFF**.

89

IT IS A MYTH THAT DOGS ONLY SEE IN BLACK AND WHITE.

DOG VISION

THEY SEE SOME COLOR, BUT NOT AS VIVIDLY AS HUMANS.

HUMAN VISION

MOST DOGS HAVE **PINK** TONGUES.

BUT CHOW CHOWS AND SHAR-PEIS HAVE **BLACK** TONGUES!

GREYHOUNDS ARE THE FASTEST DOG BREED.

THEY CAN RUN UP TO

45 MILES
(72.4 KILOMETERS)
PER HOUR!

Most dog owners give their pets GIFTS on BIRTHDAYS and SPECIAL OCCASIONS.

MOST ALSO INCLUDE THEIR PUP ON THE FAMILY HOLIDAY CARD.

SERVICE DOGS PEE AND POOP ON COMMAND!

One study says that some dogs align themselves with EARTH'S MAGNETIC FIELD while they POOP.

GEORGE WASHINGTON LOVED DOGS.

He had a **FRENCH HOUND** named **VULCAN** and a **DALMATIAN** named **MADAM MOOSE.**

THE AZTECS ONCE WORSHIPED
A HAIRLESS DOG BREED CALLED

XOLOITZCUINTLI.

(show-lo-eets-kweent-lee)

THE DOGS WERE THOUGHT
TO PROTECT HOMES
FROM EVIL SPIRITS.

Are you a fan of FANG from the *HARRY POTTER* movies?

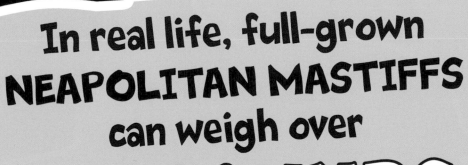

In real life, full-grown **NEAPOLITAN MASTIFFS** can weigh over

150 POUNDS

(68 KILOGRAMS)!

It is a **MYTH** that dogs feel **GUILT**.

YOUR DOG IS LIKELY FEELING **FEAR** INSTEAD.

DOG PEE CAN CORRODE METAL.

GLOSSARY

anxiety—a feeling of worry or fear

ban—to forbid something

combat—fighting between people or armies

corrode—to wear away gradually due to a chemical reaction

descendant—a person or animal who comes from a particular group of ancestors

domesticated—bred to live or work with people

honorary—given or done as a sign of honor

influential—having influence over people

instinct—behavior that is natural, rather than learned

livestock—animals kept or raised for use or pleasure, especially farm animals

membrane—a thin layer of tissue forming a barrier or lining

oxytocin—a hormone that makes humans and animals feel happy

receptor—a cell that sends signals to the sensory nerves

seizure—a sudden attack of illness that could result in a fit

territory—an area of land that an animal claims as its own to live in

vital—required for sustaining life

READ MORE

Gagne, Tammy. *Bulldogs, Poodles, Dalmations, and Other Non-Sporting Dogs.* Dog Encyclopedias. North Mankato, Minn.: Capstone Press, 2017.

Newman, Aline Alexander. *How to Speak Dog: A Guide to Decoding Dog Language.* Washington, D.C., 2013.

Sundance, Kyra. *101 Dog Tricks, Kids Edition: Fun and Easy Activities, Games, and Crafts.* Beverly, Mass.: Quarry Books, 2014.

INTERNET SITES

FactHound offers a safe, fun way to find Internet sites related to this book. All of the sites on FactHound have been researched by our staff.

Here's all you do:

Visit *www.facthound.com*

Type in this code: 9781543529258

INDEX

Mind Benders are published by Capstone,
1710 Roe Crest Drive, North Mankato, Minnesota 56003
www.mycapstone.com

Library of Congress Cataloging-in-Publication Data
Names: Potts, Nikki, author.
Title: Totally amazing facts about dogs / by Nikki Potts.
Description: North Mankato, Minnesota : an imprint of Capstone Press, [2019]
Series: Mind benders
Audience: Age 8–11.
Identifiers: LCCN 2018011013 (print)
LCCN 2018016339 (ebook)
ISBN 978-1-5435-2925-8 (hardcover)
ISBN 978-1-5435-2929-6 (paperback)
ISBN 978-1-5435-2933-3 (eBook PDF)

Subjects: LCSH: Dogs—Juvenile literature.
Classification: LCC SF426.5 (ebook)
LCC SF426.5 .P68 2019 (print)
DDC 636.7—dc23LC record available at https://lccn.loc.gov/2018011013

Printed and bound in the United States of America.
PA017

Photo Credits
Shutterstock: Victoria Rak, cover (top left), Dorottya Mathe, cover (top right), Dorottya Mathe, cover (bottom left), Kalamurzing, cover (bottom right), Javier Brosch, back cover, Dmitry Pichugin, 2, Jim Cumming, 3, Dora Zett, 4, Javier Brosch, 5, Javier Brosch, 6, vichie81, 7, Eric Isselee, 9, 10, Rickshu, 11, Patryk Kosmider, 12, Weerameth Weerachotewong, 13, Sarah Lew, 15, Dorottya Mathe, 18, M.Stasy, 18, Eric Isselee, 19, DenisNata, 20 (police dog), Talaj, 20, (police hat), Luka Djuricic, 22, otsphoto, 24 (dog side view) wavebreakmedia, 24 (girl side view), Digital Deliverance, 25, Zivica Kerkez, 26, Sonsedska Yuliia, 27, Eric Isselee, 27 (sad dog), Ermolaev Alexander, 28, Africa Studio, 29, Shevs, 30, kittipong053, 32, Dorottya Mathe, 33, Yuliya Evstratenko, 34, Javier Brosch, 35, Eric Isselee, 36, M. Unal Ozmen, 38 (popcorn), Jiri Hera, 38 (chips), Napat, 38 (paw), Ivanova N, 40, art nick, 41, Alexonline, 42, Lindsay Helms, 43, Vector_dream_team, 44, wolfness72, 45, Lena Ivanova, 46, eurobanks, 47 (dog hug), iko, 47 (doctor dog), ign, 48, Olga Kashubin, 50, Durd Yu, 51 (dog), Laborant, 51 (cake), Yezepchyk Oleksandr, 53 (Egyptian tomb), ARTSILENSE, 53 (dog), RickDeacon, 54-55 (alps), Nadezhda V. Kulagina, 54 (dog), Azuzl, 56, Blackspring, 57, Eric Isselee, 59, Illustratiostock, 61, Eric Isselee, 62 (dog), Mega Pixel, 62 (snorkel), rzoze19, 63, Dora Zett, 65, Eric Isselee, 67, MarkVanDykePhotography, 69, Jet Cat Studio, 70, Eric Isselee, 72, Annette Shaff, 73, 74-75, Ljupco Smokovski, 76, Javier Brosch, 78, Dean Drobot, 79, Nikolai Tsvetkov, 81 (ewok dog), Ryan Tanguilan, 81 (forest), Nenilkime, 82, Ermolaev Alexander, 83 (little dog), Eric Isselee, 83 (big dog), Eric Isselee, 84 (chihuahua), Csanad Kiss, 84 (dachshund), cvalle, 85 (dog), chrisbrignell, 85 (security hat), oksana2010, 88, Eric Isselee, 89, Javier Brosch, 90, 91, SikorskiFotografie, 92, Djomas, 93, Fotoeventis, 95, Ruth Black, 96, LightField Studios, 97, schubbel, 98, Everett - Art, 100 (George Washington), golfyinterlude, 100 (beagle), Eric Isselee, 100 (dalmation), Kuznetsov Alexey, 103, Erik Lam, 105, Susan Schmitz, 106, Shevs, 107 iStock/Getty Images Plus: SolStock, 64, Preto_perola, 100 (frame)

Design Elements by Shutterstock, Getty Images and DynamoLimited